W9-BXM-794

WE CAN READ about NATURE!™

FLOWERS AND FRIENDS

by ANITA HOLMES

BENCHMARK **B**OOKS

MARSHALL CAVENDISH
NEW YORK

*With thanks to
Susan Jefferson, first grade teacher at Miamitown
Elementary, Ohio, for sharing her innovative teaching
techniques in the Fun with Phonics section.*

Benchmark Books
Marshall Cavendish Corporation
99 White Plains Road
Tarrytown, New York 10591

Photo Research by Candlepants, Inc.

Cover Photo: *Animals Animals* / Bill Beatty

The photographs in this book are used by permission and through the courtesy of: *The
National Audubon Society Collection / Photo Researchers, Inc.:* Stephen Dalton, 5, 6
(top); USDA / Science Source, 6 (bottom); L. West, 7 (top); George D. Lepp, 7 (bottom);
David N. Davis, 8; Dr. Jeremy Burgess / Science Source Library, 10, 25; Darwin Dale, 11;
Steve E. Ross, 12; Dr. A.C. Twomey, 13; T. Davidson, 15; Nick Bergkessel, 17; Merlin D.
Tuttle / Bat Conservation International, 18; Richard Hutchings, 21; R.J. Erwin, 22;
Noble Proctor, 23; Walter E. Harvey, 26; Alvin E. Staffan, 27 (top); Robert Isear, 27 (bot-
tom); Margaret Miller, 28. *Animals Animals:* Jack Wilburn, 9; Bill Beatty, 14.

Library of Congress Cataloging-in-Publication Data

Holmes, Anita, date
Flowers and friends / by Anita Holmes
p. cm.– (We can read about nature!)
Includes index (p.32)
Summary: Describes the relationship among flowers and the animals necessary for
their pollination.
ISBN 0-7614-1113-5
1.Garden animals—Juvenile literature. [1. Garden animals. 2. Pollination. 3. Flowers.]
AL119.H66 2001   691.75'54—dc21   00-034268

Printed in Italy

1 3 5 6 4 2

Look for us inside this book.

bat
bumblebee
butterfly
honeybee
hummingbird
moth
ovule
pistil
pollen
stamen
wasp

I'm a fuzzy honeybee.
I'm very hungry.
Can you guess where I'm going?

I'm looking for flowers—
purple . . .

white . . .

orange . . .

and yellow.

Flowers make yellow pollen.
This is food for bees.

Flowers make sweet nectar too.
From nectar bees make honey.
All kinds of bees and wasps
like flowers.

I'm a bumblebee!

I'm a paper wasp!
We use our long tongues
to sip nectar.

Other animals like nectar too.

A cattleheart butterfly

This garden is full of butterflies.
How many can you find?

Monarch butterflies

Butterflies have long tubes for sipping nectar.

A tiger swallowtail butterfly

So do moths.
Moths visit flowers at night
after the butterflies have gone.

A tomato hornworm moth

Many flowers are shaped like tubes or cups.

Hummingbirds hover nearby.
They press their beaks into the
flowers and stick out their tongues.

A ruby-throated hummingbird

They know there is nectar inside.

Bats sleep during the day.
They hunt for food at night.

Most bats eat insects.
But this bat likes nectar.
It sticks its head right in the flower!

A lesser long-nosed bat

Many animals need flowers.
But flowers need animals too.
Animals help them make seeds.
How do they do this?

Let's take a close look
at a flower.

I have a white pistil in the middle.
Black stamens crowd all around.

Can you see the bulge
at the base of my pistil?
There are ovules inside.

Look at me!
My body is covered
with pollen.
Pollen is sticky.
When I crawl around
a flower,
I carry pollen with me.
The pollen mixes with
the ovules.
This is called pollination.

From the ovules come seeds.
And from the seeds
come flowers.

A Brazilian hummingbird

Flowers have many friends.

A common sulphur butterfly

A yellow jacket wasp

Are you a good friend to flowers?

fun with phonics

How do we become fluent readers? We interpret, or decode, the written word. Knowledge of phonics—the rules and patterns for pronouncing letters—is essential. When we come upon a word we cannot figure out by any other strategy, we need to sound out that word.

Here are some very effective tools to help early readers along their way. Use the "add-on" technique to sound out unknown words. Simply add one sound at a time, always pronouncing previous sounds. For instance, to sound out the word **cat**, first say **c**, then **c-a**, then **c-a-t**, and finally the entire word **cat**. Reading "chunks" of letters is another important skill. These are patterns of two or more letters that make one sound.

Words from this book appear below. The markings are clues to help children master phonics rules and patterns. All consonant sounds are circled. Single vowels are either long –, short ˇ, or silent /. Have fun with phonics, and a fluent reader will emerge.

Y is a consonant only when it comes at the beginning of a word.

yĕllōw   yōu

The letters "wh" make the same sound as the letter "w."

whīte   wăsps   wē

Divide compound words so the reader can identify the two smaller words that make up the compound word.

nēarbyī   īnsīde   hŭmmīngbĭrd

30

b ŭ t t e r/f l y ī   h ŏ n ē y/b ē ¢   b ŭ m b l ¢/b ē ¢

The "aw" letter combination says "all."

c r a̶w̶ l

fun facts

- A grain of pollen is so small that it can be seen only with a microscope.
- Bees are important to crops. Many farmers raise bees to help with pollination.
- Adult wasps like pollen and nectar. However, they feed caterpillars and others animal foods to their young.
- Bees usually fly in a pretty straight line from their hives to their food sources. That's where the term "beeline" comes from.
- How can you tell a moth from a butterfly? Moths have feathery antennas, or feelers. A butterfly's antennas have little knobs at the tips. When a moth is resting, it spreads its wings down flat. A butterfly folds its wings straight up. Butterflies are active during the day; moths are active at night.
- Some people plant butterfly gardens. These are gardens with special flowers that butterflies like.

glossary/index

about the author

Anita Holmes is both a writer and an editor with a long career in children's and educational publishing. She has a special interest in nature, gardening, and the environment and has written numerous articles and books for children on these subjects. A number of her books have won commendations from the American Library Association, the National Science Teachers Association, and The New York Public Library. She lives in Norfolk, Connecticut.